RAISING FISH

SARAH MACHAJEWSKI

PowerKiDS press.

New York

Published in 2020 by The Rosen Publishing Group, Inc.
29 East 21st Street, New York, NY 10010

First Edition

Editor: Tanya Dellaccio
Book Design: Michael Flynn

Photo Credits: Cover (fish) KarepaStock/Shutterstock.com; (series barn wood background) PASAKORN RANGSIYANONT/ Shutterstock.com; (series wood frame) robert_s/Shutterstock.com; cover, pp. 1, 3, 23, 24 (fish icon) MANSILIYA YURY/Shutterstock. com; p. 5 ALPA PROD/Shutterstock.com; p. 6 oneSHUTTER oneMEMORY/Shutterstock.com; p. 7 Tania Zbrodko/Shutterstock.com; p. 9 Bloomberg Creative Photos/Getty Images; p. 11 Photostravellers/Shutterstock.com; p. 12 Marius Dobilas/Shutterstock.com; p. 13 Sean Lema/Shutterstock.com; p. 14 divedog/Shutterstock.com; p. 15 Ventura/Shutterstock.com; p. 17 © iStockphoto.com/ commablack; p. 18 Kazakova Maryia/Shutterstock.com; p. 19 Zykov_Vladimir/Shutterstock.com; p. 21 Liz O. Baylen/Los Angeles Times/Getty Images; p. 22 Edward Westmacott/Shutterstock.com.

Cataloging-in-Publication Data

Names: Machajewski, Sarah.
Title: Raising fish / Sarah Machajewski.
Description: New York : PowerKids Press, 2020. | Series: Unusual farm animals | Includes glossary and index.
Identifiers: ISBN 9781725308985 (pbk.) | ISBN 9781725309005 (library bound) | ISBN 9781725308992 (6 pack)
Subjects: LCSH: Fish culture–Juvenile literature. | Fisheries–Juvenile literature. | Fishes–Juvenile literature.
Classification: LCC SH151.M33 2020 | DDC 639.3–dc23

Manufactured in the United States of America

CPSIA Compliance Information: Batch #CWPK20. For Further Information contact Rosen Publishing, New York, New York at 1-800-237-9932.

CONTENTS

FISH ON THE FARM 4

WHAT IS AQUACULTURE? 6

FRESHWATER FARMING 8

FARMING IN THE SALTY SEAS 10

TYPES OF FISH FARMS 12

ALL ABOUT SHELLFISH FARMING 14

FISH FARMING BASICS 16

THE FISH LIFE CYCLE 18

SHELLFISH STAGES 20

FISH OF THE FUTURE 22

GLOSSARY 23

INDEX 24

WEBSITES 24

FISH ON THE FARM

Fish live in the ocean, in other bodies of water, and in tanks in our homes. Did you know they live on farms, too? Fish may seem out of place on a farm, but they're just as important as other farm animals. They provide food for people around the world.

Farmers all over the country and the world raise fish. They require special farming **technology** and a lot of care.

HOW UNUSUAL!

Fish farming is the fastest growing area of food **production**.

LIFE ON THE FARM ISN'T JUST FOR CHICKENS, PIGS, OR COWS. FISH CAN BE FARM ANIMALS, TOO!

WHAT IS AQUACULTURE?

"Agriculture" is another word for farming. Fish farming is called aquaculture. People raise fish and **shellfish** on special farms. These farms can be in natural waterways, such as oceans. Man-made fish farms can be inside buildings. There may even be one in your city or town!

SHELLFISH FARM

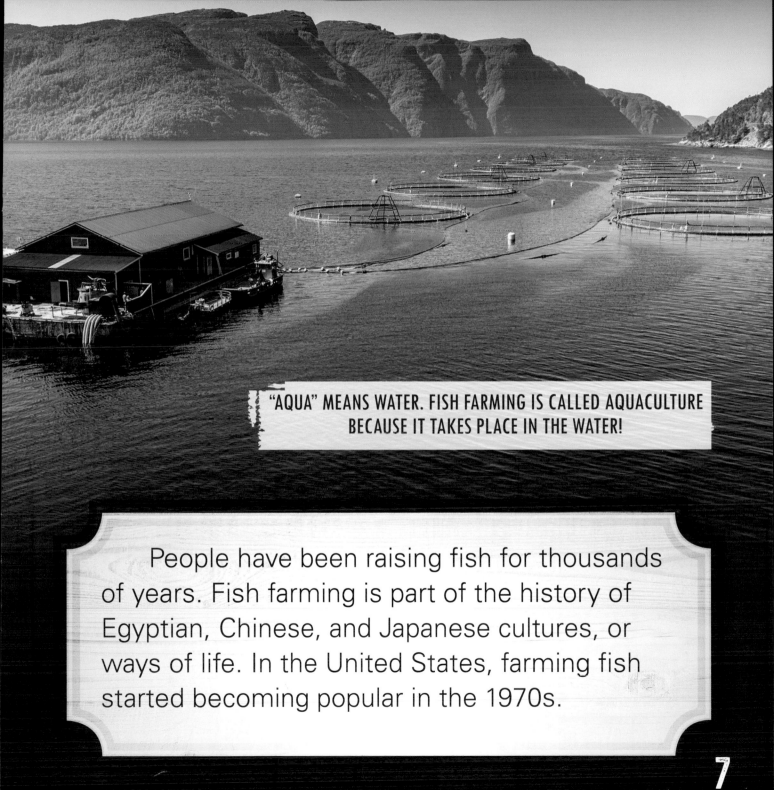

"AQUA" MEANS WATER. FISH FARMING IS CALLED AQUACULTURE BECAUSE IT TAKES PLACE IN THE WATER!

People have been raising fish for thousands of years. Fish farming is part of the history of Egyptian, Chinese, and Japanese cultures, or ways of life. In the United States, farming fish started becoming popular in the 1970s.

FRESHWATER FARMING

Fish farmers raise many kinds of fish and shellfish. The places where they raise fish depend on what type of water the fish need to live in. Some fish need freshwater **habitats**. Freshwater farms are built in ponds, rivers, and lakes. Some are man-made.

Trout and carp are the most commonly farmed freshwater fish. Together, they make up about 70 percent of all freshwater aquaculture. Other species, or kinds, of freshwater fish include striped bass, tilapia, and yellow perch.

HOW UNUSUAL!

We **consume** so much tilapia that some people call it "aqua-chicken" after the other popular farm animal.

THIS CATFISH WAS RAISED ON A FRESHWATER FARM IN ALABAMA. FULL-GROWN CATFISH WEIGH BETWEEN ONE AND TWO POUNDS (0.5 TO 0.9 KG).

FARMING IN THE SALTY SEAS

Many kinds of fish live in saltwater habitats such as the ocean. Marine aquaculture is farming those fish and shellfish that live in the ocean.

In the United States, marine aquaculture makes up about 20 percent of all fish farming. **Marine** aquaculture takes place both in the ocean and in man-made tanks on land. Farmers raise many shellfish species on these farms, including mussels, oysters, and clams. They also raise some kinds of salmon and shrimp.

HOW UNUSUAL!

Some fish travels a long way to get to the grocery store. About 90 percent of farm-raised seafood comes from Asia.

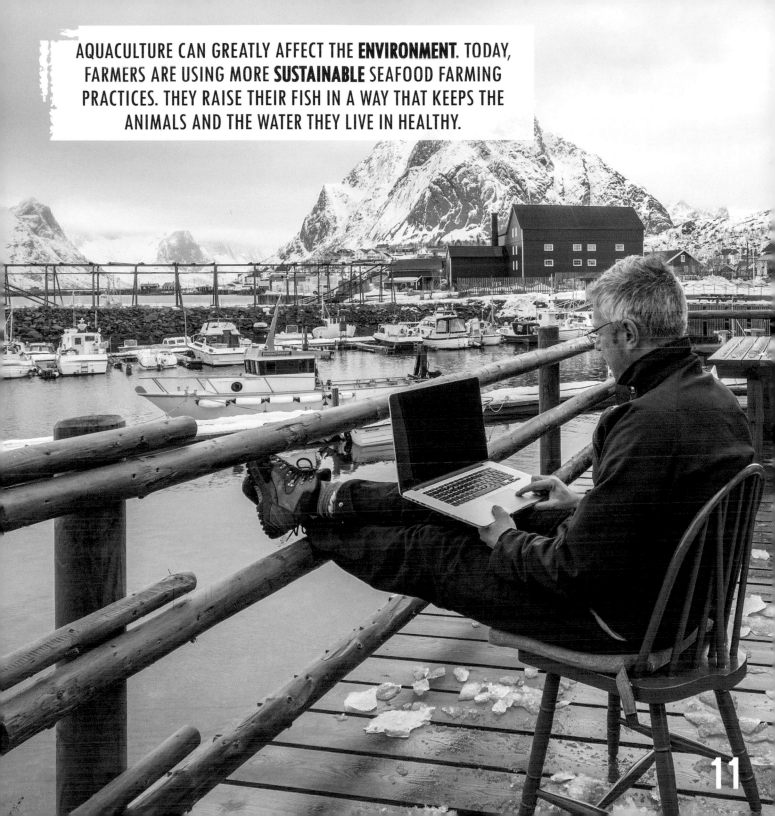

AQUACULTURE CAN GREATLY AFFECT THE **ENVIRONMENT**. TODAY, FARMERS ARE USING MORE **SUSTAINABLE** SEAFOOD FARMING PRACTICES. THEY RAISE THEIR FISH IN A WAY THAT KEEPS THE ANIMALS AND THE WATER THEY LIVE IN HEALTHY.

TYPES OF FISH FARMS

Just like on farms on land, there's a wide range of technology and tools for farming in the water. Farmers raise fish in many different kinds of environments, including pens or nets. They even use tanks on land.

NET PEN

HOW UNUSUAL!

How do farmers keep their watery farms in order? Sometimes they use robot fish! These machines often look like real fish and are placed in fish farms, where they "swim" and watch conditions. Some robot fish can even help clean the underwater habitat!

RACEWAY SYSTEM

Net pens are placed entirely underwater in oceans or other large waterways. Ponds are another type of **enclosure**. They can be natural or built next to rivers and lakes. A raceway is a canal, or channel, that's built to have water constantly flowing in and out.

ALL ABOUT SHELLFISH FARMING

The methods used to farm shellfish are a little different. Bottom culture farming is one method. Farmers set up raised beds in areas with shallow water. The shellfish grow on the beds, and farmers harvest, or gather, them when they're ready.

Off-bottom culture is another way to raise shellfish. These systems don't sit on the bottom of the ocean floor. Instead, ropes float near the surface, and the shellfish attach to them in long **columns**.

OFF-BOTTOM CULTURE

BOTTOM CULTURE FARMING ISN'T JUST FOR SHELLFISH. FARMERS ALSO GROW SEAWEED USING THIS METHOD.

15

FISH FARMING BASICS

Farming requires care, attention, planning, and knowledge. Every plant and animal has different needs. Farmers must know how to care for these needs. That's how they raise animals and plants that are healthy and strong.

The methods farmers use to raise fish depend on the needs of the kind of fish they're raising. Knowing what kind of water different fish need to live in is the first step in starting a fish farm. Fish may need fresh water or salt water, and they may need cold water or warm **temperatures**.

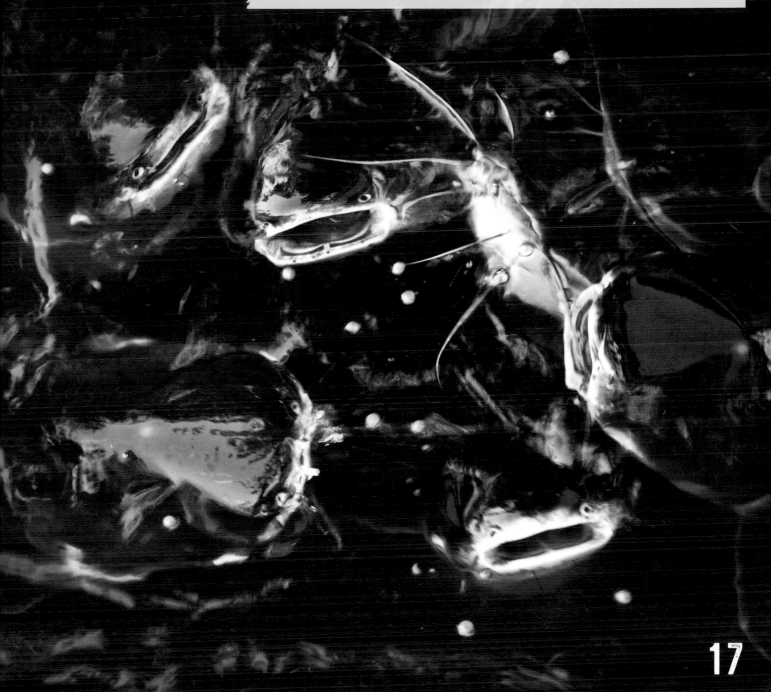

FARMERS NEED TO KNOW WHAT TO FEED THEIR FISH. SOME FISH ARE SCAVENGERS, WHICH MEANS THEY EAT ANYTHING THEY COME ACROSS. OTHERS EAT ONLY PLANTS. SOME FISH WILL ONLY EAT OTHER FISH!

THE FISH LIFE CYCLE

Farmers need to know everything about the animals they raise. Fish farmers care for fish through all stages of their life cycle, or all the changes they go through as they grow.

HERE'S A LOOK AT HOW FARMERS RAISE FISH FROM THE TIME THEY'RE EGGS UNTIL THEY'RE ADULTS.

FARMING FISH FROM EGG TO ADULT

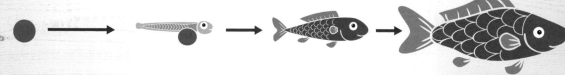

EGG

FARMERS KEEP THOUSANDS OF EGGS IN HATCHERIES, OR SPECIAL PLACES THAT HOLD EGGS, UNTIL THEY'RE BORN.

LARVA

FARMERS MOVE THEIR FISH LARVAE TO FRESH, CLEAN WATER. THERE, THE FISH ARE FED AND CARED FOR UNTIL THEY GET BIGGER.

JUVENILE

FARMERS TAKE JUVENILE FISH TO A BIGGER PEN, NET, OR TANK. SOME FISH TRAVEL BY TRUCK TO THEIR FARM IN THE OCEAN!

ADULT

FARMERS FEED AND CARE FOR THEIR FISH UNTIL THE FISH ARE FULL GROWN. THEN, THE FISH ARE HARVESTED FOR FOOD OR USED TO MAKE NEW FISH.

A fish begins life in an egg. It usually hatches, or comes out of the egg, several days after it's laid. Next is the larval stage. After this, fish enter the **juvenile** stage. Juvenile fish look a lot like adult fish. Fish enter the adult stage when they can reproduce, or make new fish.

SHELLFISH STAGES

Farmers who raise oysters, clams, or other shellfish need to have specialized skills and knowledge. That's because shellfish live and grow differently than other fish.

Adult shellfish release thousands of tiny cells that join together and make shellfish larvae. The larvae float in the water. Then, they attach to a hard surface under the water where they grow and develop their hard outer shell. On farms, shellfish are stacked into tall columns or placed in cages. As shellfish grow, farmers move them to larger cages.

HOW UNUSUAL!

Oysters in the larvae stage are called "spat."

MANY OYSTER FARMERS START OFF BY BUYING SPAT. WHY? THEIR WATERS MAY NOT BE WARM ENOUGH FOR SHELLFISH TO PRODUCE SPAT ON THEIR OWN. THIS IS ONE WAY FARMERS HAVE ADAPTED TO THE CONDITIONS IN THEIR ENVIRONMENT.

FISH OF THE FUTURE

Aquaculture is a growing business that shows no signs of slowing down. People all over the world are buying and eating more farm-raised fish than ever before. In fact, we now eat as much farm-raised seafood as seafood that's caught in the wild.

What does this mean for farmers? They must balance the needs of their business with the effect it has on the environment. As farmers come up with newer, better, and safer practices, our seafood—and our seas—will be cleaner and healthier.

column: Something tall and thin in shape.

consume: Eat or drink.

enclosure: An area that is sealed off.

environment: The natural world around us.

habitat: The natural home for plants, animals, and other living things.

juvenile: An animal that is older than a baby and younger than an adult.

marine: Having to do with the sea.

production: The process of making something.

shellfish: An animal, such as a crab or oyster, that lives in water and has a hard outer shell.

sustainable: Able to be used without being completely used up or destroyed.

technology: A method that uses science to solve problems and the tools used to solve those problems.

temperature: How hot or cold something is.

INDEX

B
bass, striped, 8
bottom culture farming, 14, 15

C
carp, 8
catfish, 9
clams, 10, 20

M
mussels, 10

N
nets, 12, 13, 18

O
off-bottom culture, 14

oysters, 10, 20, 21

P
pens, 12, 13, 18
perch, yellow, 8

R
raceway, 13

S
salmon, 10
shellfish, 6, 8, 10, 14, 15, 20, 21
shrimp, 10

T
tilapia, 8
trout, 8

WEBSITES

Due to the changing nature of Internet links, PowerKids Press has developed an online list of websites related to the subject of this book. This site is updated regularly. Please use this link to access the list: www.powerkidslinks.com/ufa/fish